INTERACTIVE STEP-BY-STEPS TO
SPITFIRE SUCCESS IN BOTH

GREAT
SMALL
BUSINESS
GREAT
BIG
LIFE

HOLLY GEORGE

authorHOUSE®

AuthorHouse™
1663 Liberty Drive
Bloomington, IN 47403
www.authorhouse.com
Phone: 1 (800) 839-8640

www.spitfirepromotiongroup.com

Published by AuthorHouse 10/17/2017

ISBN: 978-1-5462-0998-0 (sc)
ISBN: 978-1-5462-0997-3 (e)

Library of Congress Control Number: 2017914854

Print information available on the last page.

This book is printed on acid-free paper.

CONTENTS

Chapter 1: Find Fun Again 1

Chapter 2: Get Organized...9

Chapter 3: Raise Supportive Kids (and spouses) 19

Chapter 4: Create More Money and Your Passion for Making It ...29

Chapter 5: Check Your Systems.....................................39

Chapter 6: Write Your Plan for Unstoppable Success....................47

PREMISE

"You seriously should write a sit-com!"

If I had a dime for every time I heard that, I wouldn't need to write anything… I'd be sitting on a remote beach with a witness-protected alias and 50 million in an off-shore account. Let's just say my family is f@#ked up… in a good way, of course.

We're Greek* so we're loud and we'll tell you exactly what we think (whether you ask or not). In other words, we don't hide behind the truth; we sock you in the nuts with it. But we are right. Just ask us.

* *I'm technically not Greek, but my husband is 100%, and once you've lived with that for 25+ years you've earned the right. Plus, my mother-in-law always reminds me that I'm "Greek by injection." (Oy!)*

Here's a little sitcom scenario to prove my point. My husband, a medical sales rep at the time, loaded our grill and all the supplies for Greek Chicken in the back of his pickup, to provide an authentic lunch for a bunch of physicians. His parents were visiting, so he grabbed his dad (a fantastic cook) and headed off to one of his best accounts, a large hospital. While my husband was inside setting up, my father-in-law grilled amazing Greek chicken in the hospital parking lot. They didn't pre-think the notion that there might be a couple stray dogs in the area, so when they showed up begging, he had to keep pushing them away. Easy enough. But then he didn't have anyone to guard the grill when he got the urge! So, logic said pee in the grass just around the corner with the grill sizzling in the background... duh. (Logic was invented by Greeks, so this makes it okay.) Fortunately, my husband showed up to man the grill and fend off dogs in time for him to run inside and wash his hands before he touched anything.

(This was back in the 90's, people... back when there was no social media to "share" an opinion on this being gross, so just laugh.)

"What's your secret?"

That's the comment that quickly follows the 'sit-com' comment... and it's the real reason I'm writing this book. I didn't start out with the habits for great health, finances and happiness. I had to figure them out.

My "Secrets" are simple:

1. You must challenge yourself.

My grandfather, Les Chaffin (who fell to Alzheimer's), always challenged me to grow financially. He bought a fledgling business and built it up, hated paying taxes, and took advantage of every write-off within the law. He would say "It's not what you do from 9:00 — 5:00 that matters most. It's what you do from 5:00 — 9:00." In other words, those who put forth more effort, get more. I like to think this also meant "work smart." However, this is the same man who always told me "I'd love to buy you for what you're really worth, and sell you for what you think you're worth."

My father-in-law, Jim George (who was never the same after his heart attack) read people better than anyone (my husband, David, is a very close second, btw). He could meet you and peg you with 99% accuracy as successful, an idiot, a bum, insincere... the list is long. I learned from him to shut up and listen, trust my instincts, and act accordingly. (Yes, this is Mr. Parking Lot Pee.)

2. You must take risks.

My mom (who died after several brain surgeries) taught me "you've got to spend it to get it." And, boy, could she spend money. On some really stupid stuff. But she also got her real estate license after my sister and I were in high school. She earned additional certifications, bought land, subdivided it, and developed it for profit.

My friend and financial advisor, Nancy Anderson, challenged me to truly diversify when investing. I'll never forget the day she told me "I won't take any more of your money. You need to do something else." She encouraged me to expand to other investments, and it opened a large door.

3. You must stay grounded.

My dad taught me to not sweat the small stuff. My dad doesn't really sweat the big stuff either, but, oh well. My dad is a very grounded and reliable guy. I remember him ripping a borrowed Judy Blume book titled "Forever" in half when he found out I was reading it after being told not to. (Remember Judy Blume's old-school porn for teens, ladies?) My dad taught me that no matter how big I think I am, there's always bigger. I'll always have to earn respect and follow rules.

I'm what you'd consider a Driver/Type A/High D/(dare I admit) selfish person. I can get so focused on tasks that I neglect feelings. My kids help me remember this daily. Like when they say "what's for dinner?" at 6 p.m., and I haven't even started to cook. Of course I love them, but this ultra-focus that I can't seem to shatter is a big reason why I will bawl when all my kids have moved out and I'll wonder where the time went.

4. You must be real.

When I said "yes" to David George, I knew that that he was going to be a daily handful. I knew I'd marry David on our second date, when he leaned over to an ancient lady before watching a Marvin Hamlisch concert at the Minneapolis Symphony (got the tickets as a gift from my dad... don't ask), and inquired "About how long is this thing supposed to last?" She cracked up. David is funny, heart-felt, candid (aka Greek), and arguably THE biggest challenge anyone could encounter. He taught me to have an opinion, and don't be afraid to use it. The people who don't like it were never in your corner anyway. He will hands-down make you a better person (if you are willing to put up with his crap).

Don't dance around issues. Say "no" when you should. When asked for your opinion, be honest. (Not cruel, but honest.) Be a parent — not a friend — to your kids.

All this raw realism will get you in trouble sometimes, but the benefits outweigh the risks. That's when I remind myself that I'm one of the most heartfelt people I know. I cry at weddings. I tear up whenever our National Anthem is played. And I choke up on Senior parents' nights. And when my kids are truly struggling or hurt (not being lazy or looking for sympathy), I'm their biggest advocate and will work tirelessly to help find solutions.

5. Coffee and excellent red wine.

Rev up your day, and unwind at night. No explanation necessary.

> *"Life should not be a journey to the grave with the intention of arriving safely in an attractive and well-preserved body... but rather to skid in sideways, chocolate in one hand, martini in the other, body totally worn out and screaming... 'WOO HOO — What A Ride!'"*
>
> ~ *Author Unknown, but Brilliant*

I tell you all this because it's important to know and respect the people you take advice from. This book is full of tried and true advice, along with some very personal anecdotes that back my advice. I've incorporated into this book the major step-by-steps that worked for me to establish excellent habits that have allowed me to take my business and life from $5 per hour intern to healthy, happy and very comfortable. Each chapter lays out customizable "Step-by-Steps" - steps that worked for me, and have worked for my clients since 1994 - in interactive workbook format, "Quick Tips," and "Be A Spitfire" shots in the arm.

Enjoy your journey, and know that I welcome your stories and encourage your feedback: www.SpitfirePromotionGroup.com.

Chapter 1

Find Fun Again

Watch your kids play. If you don't have kids, watch your friends' kids play. Kids are always happy at play. They always make time for play. Why don't adults? What makes you happy? Do that. Today.

Do you like coffee or tea? How about therapeutic massage? Pilates? Swimming? Shopping and lunch with a friend? Basketball lunches? Reading? Writing? Rithmetic?

Many adults simply don't take time to do what they love most. Many haven't done anything for themselves in so long that they don't know what they love any more. They've forgotten how to play.

It's important to do what makes you happy. And the sooner you establish a routine of doing what you love, the sooner you'll be able to carry a new happiness into all your relationships and everything you do… namely your business.

Now, let's find out what makes you happy (I call these your Sanity Preservers), and how to insert these Sanity Preservers into your life.

Discovering and Enjoying Your Sanity Preservers

1. Schedule 20 minutes of quiet time.

2. Grab a pen.

3. Set a timer for 5 minutes, and write a list of things that make —
or would make — you happy. Nothing is incorrect. You may include
everything from skiing the Alps to combing your daughter's hair.
Write for the entire 5 minutes. Imagine favorite people, scenes, scents,
tastes, climates and sounds. Dream. Go where your mind takes you,
and keep writing.

_____

_____

_____

_____

_____

_____

_____

_____

_____

_____

_____

_____

4. Organize your list by placing each item on your list onto one of 5 smaller lists:

• Things I could do daily

_____

_____

_____

_____

_____

_____

• Things I could do weekly

_____

_____

_____

_____

_____

_____

- Things I could do monthly

_____

_____

_____

_____

_____

- Things I could do occasionally

_____

_____

_____

_____

_____

- Things I strive to accomplish

_____

_____

_____

_____

_____

5. Prioritize your lists:

- Start with your "daily" list, and rank the top 5 things you could start doing today.

    1. _____

    2. _____

    3. _____

    4. _____

    5. _____

- Move on to your "weekly" list, and rank the top 3 things you could start doing this week.

    1. _____

    2. _____

    3. _____

- On your "monthly" list, rank the top 2 things you could start doing this month.

    1. _____

    2. _____

- Next, on your "occasionally" list, rank the top 5 things you could do soon.

    1. _____

    2. _____

3. _____

4. _____

5. _____

• Finally, on your "strive to accomplish" list, don't rank anything. Leave it alone.

6. Take action:

• Do the 3 of the 5 things on your "daily" list today. And tomorrow. And the next day. And the day after that. Establish a routine of doing 3-5 things just for you every day. They may vary slightly, but the more consistent you are day-to-day, the more likely you will be to stick to this new rule.

For example, every day I do this: exercise for 1 hour in the morning; drink my afternoon coffee; flirt with David; relax for 30 minutes before bed. Every day. Home and away.

I knew I'd done a good job of establishing a good sanity preserving routine for myself when my (at the time) 4-year-old daughter piped up from the back seat while on vacation and pulling into Starbucks: "Are you going to get your latte now, Mommy?" (Yikes!)

• Do one of the top 3 things on your "weekly" list this week. And next week. And the week after that. Establish a routine of doing at least one of the top 3 items on your list every week. Don't deviate from this new rule. Schedule it a week in advance.

Every week, I either schedule alone time (lunch or coffee) with a friend, go to the salon (get a haircut, massage, facial, wax... the list gets longer every year), or clean out a drawer, cupboard, etc. Every week.

- Do one of the top 2 things on your "monthly" list this month. And next month. You get the idea.

  So you remember to do it, leave yourself a reminder. If you want to do a pedicure this month, leave a bottle of nail polish laying on your bathroom vanity as a reminder. Then you'll remember to treat yourself when time allows. If you want to play a round of golf, put your clubs in your trunk and a golf ball in your car's drink holder as a reminder.

- Post your "occasionally" list in your closet. While you're getting dressed, mull over when you could work one of your occasional items into your schedule sometime soon.

- Finally, keep your "strive to accomplish" list next to your bed. Consult this list before you turn out the lights.

Your new lists will teach you how to play again. They'll train you to take care of yourself and to dream bigger. And all this striving and newfound happiness just may push you to accomplish something on that big dream list!

Be A Spitfire

**Here are some more "musts" for
achieving a happy and fun attitude.**

Love your husband.

Put on a smile. Don't sweat the small stuff. Flirt,
and be his girlfriend. The "man code" is basic:
feed 'em, f@#k 'em, and tell 'em they're great.
(And mean it, of course.)

Laugh with your kids.

Ugh! I feel like I can be such a nagging drag at
times. I have to remind myself daily that I'm
raising adults that hopefully will choose to spend
time with ME over their crazy in-laws. I better turn
up the fun.

Connect with core friends.

Notice I say "core friends," because not
everybody is a bestie. Get off Facebook or
whatever else sucks your precious time. Surround
yourself with positive people who encourage you
to move forward. People who do the right thing.
People who like to have fun and allow you to
express yourself genuinely. If your friends don't fit
this description, dump them. I call this "cleaning
house," and I've done it. It's liberating, as both of
you are able to fill a new void with someone who
is a better match.

Chapter 2

Get Organized

Now that you're more fun than ever, let's find time to play! Establish your core routine and liberating schedule.

Before you dream big about your family of five basking in the Arabian sun on a business write-off vacation (or dream smaller about simply sitting down to dinner together every night at 7:00), there is one fundamental task to be addressed: scheduling.

Family and personal issues should be given utmost importance in your hectic schedule, so this chapter addresses the best way to be sure this happens.

Before the first consideration of growing a business and making work commitments, master the basics:

1.   Your Core Daily Routine

        A good core daily routine puts family and personal commitments first.

2.   Your Weekly Planner

        A planner that offers a week-at-a-glance is ideal. It allows enough room to record all types of daily appointments while still displaying your entire week for quick reference.

Quick Tip

Get yourself a good planner. I like Flintstone-era spiral binders that hold 5.5" x 8.5" replacement pages that I purchase every year at any office store. I've found that this one-week-at-a-glance is ideal for me to schedule work, family and personal tasks all in one place. If you prefer your computer or handheld, use that. The scheduling advice in this chapter is easily adapted to any medium.

Establishing Your Core Daily Routine

First, let's establish your core daily routine.

A daily routine is crucial to a happy family and personal life. Here's how you can establish a routine very simply.

1. Schedule 20 minutes of quiet time.

2. Grab two pens — each a different color.

3. With one pen, write down the events throughout your family's day that you feel are important to experience together. Write these things below, next to the time that each takes place. (See the example

below, and then use the blank day provided after it to write your own schedule.)

Example:	
6:00 A.M.	
7:00 A.M.	**Breakfast**
8:00 A.M.	
9:00 A.M.	
10:00 A.M.	
11:00 A.M.	
12:00 P.M.	
1:00 P.M.	
2:00 P.M.	
3:00 P.M.	
4:00 P.M.	**Kids Home from School**
5:00 P.M.	
6:00 P.M.	**Dinner**
7:00 P.M.	
8:00 P.M.	
9:00 P.M.	**Kids Bedtime**
10:00 P.M.	
11:00 P.M.	

Your Day: _____

6:00 A.M. _____

7:00 A.M. _____

8:00 A.M. _____

9:00 A.M. _____

10:00 A.M. _____

11:00 A.M. _____

12:00 P.M. _____

1:00 P.M. _____

2:00 P.M. _____

3:00 P.M. _____

4:00 P.M. _____

5:00 P.M. _____

6:00 P.M. _____

7:00 P.M. _____

8:00 P.M. _____

9:00 P.M. _____

10:00 P.M. _____

11:00 P.M. _____

4. In a different color ink, go back and fill in your routine. Don't forget to write down your daily Sanity Preservers. Record specific times if possible.

Example:	
6:00 A.M.	Exercise
7:00 A.M.	**Breakfast**
8:00 A.M.	
9:00 A.M.	
10:00 A.M.	
11:00 A.M.	
12:00 P.M.	Take Vitamins
1:00 P.M.	
2:00 P.M.	Soy Latte
3:00 P.M.	
4:00 P.M.	**Kids Home from School**
5:00 P.M.	
6:00 P.M.	**Dinner**
7:00 P.M.	
8:00 P.M.	
9:00 P.M.	**Kids Bedtime**
10:00 P.M.	Alone Time
11:00 P.M.	

5. Post this routine on your refrigerator.

6. Follow it.

You can see how establishing a good core daily routine accomplishes 3 very important things:

> 1. Gives your family a blueprint for knowing when sacred, non-negotiable together time is scheduled;
>
> 2. Solidifies the importance of family in the minds of the people you love the most;
>
> 3. Shows you a clear path for fitting work into your life.

Now that you've established a core daily routine that works for your family, it's time to organize your life.

Establishing your weekly planner.

Do you see the gaps and opportune times in your daily routine? This is where you have room to schedule work and play. Let's look at your planner. Since you're committed to religiously following your core daily routine, it's time to write it into your planner. Then, you'll fill in your planner pages with other commitments.

A sample day is provided at the end of this exercise.

1. Get a planner. Again, I recommend spiral binders that hold 5.5" x 8.5" replacement pages that can bepurchased every year at any office store. One week-at-a-glance is ideal for scheduling work, family and personal tasks all in one place.

2. When planning for the upcoming week, commit to recording your core daily routine onto every day first.

3.   Add any non-routine, scheduled family commitments.

4.   Write in any work and other commitments under the correct day and time.

5.   Underline or circle the time to the left of each commitment that is scheduled at a specific time, so it's obvious at-a-glance that these are planned appointments.

6.   Write in your weekly Sanity Preservers.

Quick Tip

To honor one of your non-scheduled, weekly Sanity Preservers (like play a round of golf), make a note in the margin at the top of the week.

If you need to simply remind your spouse of an appointment that doesn't really involve you, or if you want to call your mother to ask how her doctor's appointment went, put this task in parentheses.

7.   Next to any task that involves remembering something to take with you, place an asterisk.

8.   At the bottom of the day, record any unscheduled tasks that you want to get done that day as a list of "things to do."

If you're the family shopper, establish one separate location for your grocery and other store lists. Place an asterisk next to your "Errands" entry in your things to do list, so you remember to grab these shopping lists when you're heading out the door (see sample day below).

Example:

(Tommy – remember to wear cowboy hat for western day at school.)

6:00 A.M.	Exercise
7:00 A.M.	**Breakfast**
8:00 A.M.	
8:30	(David take car in for oil change)
9:00 A.M.	
10:00 A.M.	
11:00 A.M.	
12:00 P.M.	Lunch at Spaggio with Lori / **Take Vitamins**
1:00 P.M.	Elena take medicine before nap
2:00 P.M.	**Soy Latte**
2:30	Mack to Dr. Barker
3:00 P.M.	Errands
4:00 P.M.	**Kids Home from School**
5:00 P.M.	
6:00 P.M.	Dinner at Carlsons (take dessert & gift)*
7:00 P.M.	
8:00 P.M.	
9:00 P.M.	**Kids Bedtime**
10:00 P.M.	**Alone Time**
11:00 P.M.	

Things To Do:

• Wrap gift

• Call about car insurance

• Pay bills

• Tommy write paper

• Groceries *

Quick Tip

Get in the habit of recording every little thing that needs to be done in your planner – even if it's as simple as grocery shopping.

Cross out tasks when they're ~~done~~. This will give you a great sense of accomplishment at the end of the day and week. However, don't cross them out to the point of illegibility, as you may want to look back later to remember when an appointment or task took place.

A good planner incorporates your core routine and gives you a completely organized, birdseye view of your day and week. It identifies your free time, streamlines your day, and unclutters your mind. It reveals where you have time to add in work tasks. It liberates and empowers you. It changes your life!

Be A Spitfire

Play the "10 Things" Game.

Open a drawer, and throw away 10 things. Or look at the pile of clothes on your floor, and hang up 10 things. Look at your cluttered office and put away 10 things.

You get the idea. It's addicting. You'll find yourself looking for areas in your home to play this game.

This is a great game to boost your sanity... even if you have only a spare minute.

Chapter 3

Raise Supportive Kids (and spouses)

If you don't have kids, a spouse, or significant other, you can skip this chapter and come back to it later. Or read it, so you know what NOT to do should you decide to add these things into your life!

You're now fun and organized, and you're one more step toward energizing yourself to catapult your business or career to the next level. It's important that your kids help out and that you encourage your spouse to support your new rockstar attitude.

Since you plan to grow a business that will be reflected in you and those you choose to hang with, it's important that your family has some basic skills mastered. Would you buy gourmet cookies from a gal with a dirty house? How about laying out money for a parenting seminar from a guy with whiny kids? When owning a business, image matters.

Let's start with the kids.

Manners and work ethic in this crazy age of entitlement and working the system seem to be a dying art. Do we raise our kids to do the right thing? Or do we teach them how to work the system, so they don't get screwed?

I've witnessed my kids being treated unfairly for totally ridiculous reasons. Of course we raise them to do the right things. And when they get screwed, we're honest with them, saying: "That's a great life lesson. You don't always get what's fair. And you need to learn to deal with all kinds of people. Even the idiots."

It's amazing to me how many families don't communicate that simple fact with their kids. Or other simple facts, like if you smoke or drink, I'll jack you up against the wall so hard you won't be able to inhale or swallow for weeks. Or if you pierce or tattoo anything while you're in my house or living on my dime, you better be ready to fully support yourself on your own. Done. These are our house rules… yours may be different, of course. But you get my point.

Or how about this one… if someone bullies you or one of your friends, go ahead and take a swing at them, and make it count. I guarantee they'll never do it again. If you are right, we will always back you up. But you better be right. How's that for an anti-bullying program?

It's very important to note that our house is faaaaaaar from perfect. (Remember how I said my family was f@#ked up… in a good way?) My kids hear the "F" word (my favorite) and other swearing from us. However, they know they aren't allowed to say these things until they are legal adults. Beyond 18, we tell them that if they think it's a good idea, let it fly. (They do occasionally say things like "freakin'" and "effin," though. Oh well, we'll take that over a C, D or F.)

Kids used to fear their parents at least a little. So many today do not. Such a shame.

Quick Tip

No iPods or cell phones in young kids' bedrooms during school nights. There's really no need, and they're such a time-suck! My kids do get them on the weekends if they've got A's and are rocking it in their sports and extras.

This rule started when I walked into Mack's (my middle child... I could write an entire book on just him) room one middle school evening to see him rapidly clicking and scrolling:

Mom: "What are you doing?"

Mack: "Liking photos."

Mom: "Oh? Show me what you like about them."

We went through each of the 175 "friends" photos and discussed what he liked about each one. For most of them he had no particular reason... especially the piece of pizza that one of his "friends" posted. (That was my personal favorite.)

Mom: "Let's make your 'likes' count from now on. And, no more phones in rooms."

Mack: "Okay. That's actually probably a good idea because it's a distraction anyway."

(Really? Geez!)

Boys and girls should be taught basic "old school" lessons, as these dying art lessons are what will make them stand out in today's era of "look-at-me-selfie-taking-video-posting-I-do-nothing-special-but-I've-been-told-my-whole-life-that-I'm-great-and-I-got-trophies-just-for-showing-up." (My kids either gave those back or threw them away.)

Lay down rules, and consistently enforce them (something my husband is waaay better at than I am… I mean sometimes it's hard to remember if I shaved my pits, let alone who's got what taken away for how long). Don't engage in arguments with your kids. Be consistent. Love them through it all, and you'll have great kids. No matter how pissed I am at them or how much they screwed up on any given day, I kiss my kids goodnight every night.

Learning the "Standout Kid" Essentials

Prepare your kids for any life situation as best you can. There are things kids should just know.

<u>Manners, Babe</u>

I always got compliments on my kids' manners when they were little. This is so easy to teach. Pound the basics into their heads by not responding unless they use them. Enough repetition with this, and you'll have it nailed for life in no time.

Here is a checklist of the basics, and they should be used in every situation:

_____   "Yes, please."

_____   "No, thank you."

_____   "Excuse me."

_____ Open doors for people. (And hold the door when you're going through.)

_____ Help the elderly. (We've pulled the car over before, so my son could get out and take the shovel from an 80-year-old that was shoveling her sidewalk. It took him 1/10 the time it would have taken her, and he withstands 10° northern Wisconsin weather much more readily.)

Proper Handshake

Role play the right and wrong way to meet someone and hold a conversation. Make this silly and fun by exaggerating wrong things and acting overtly proper with the right things.

Here's the sequence:

1. Walk up to the person, smiling and making eye contact.
2. Extend your right hand preparing to handshake.
3. Start shaking their hand firmly (but not too firm), saying "Hi. I'm Tommy George. It's nice to meet you."
4. Continue to make eye contact as you carry on conversation and act genuinely interested.

I'm known to ridicule even an adult bad handshake. Don't let your kid be one of the casualties.

Dining & Setting a Table

Play a Memory Game with a formal table setting. So what if you don't have time to dine this way at home (even though you should try to occasionally) or the money to drag them to five-stars. We all secretly hope they will need this skill some day.

Set a place at your table using several dishes and utensils. (If you're not aware of proper placement, just Google it.) Teach your kids what each piece is used for. Explain that the reason for each piece's placement is that you typically eat "from the outside, in." For example, salad is served before dinner, which is why the salad plate is on top of the dinner plate and the salad fork is outside the dinner fork. Let your kids study the placement for a minute, then disassemble the place setting. Have them reset it, telling you the name of each piece as they do this.

Napkins go in laps. Chew with your mouth closed. Don't interrupt. Pass food to the right (counterclockwise).

One of my proudest moments was when Mack came home and told me they had a fun test on table setting at school, and he was the only one that got them all right! (I know, my priorities may be outta whack a little. Fast forward to him in a business lunch interview, "liking" dumb business ideas, but he gets the job because he stood out by knowing what the bread plate was for. Good boy.)

<u>Fight for What's Right</u>

Letting your kids fight their own battles prepares them for dealing with confrontation in any situation, empowering them with experience to draw on as issues get bigger in their lifetime. Most importantly, they know that the success they realize after dealing with a heart-pounding issue is all theirs to celebrate.

Talk about the tough situation with your child, and figure out options they can use for responses. Choose the best tactic, and have them role play with you. Practice. Practice. Practice. Remind them that you've been there and had big butterflies, too. It gets easier.

The worst that can happen is nothing. Teach them that it's always better to deal with the situation. They may not be able to control outcomes, but they can control their reactions and resulting decisions. What a powerful lesson!

Lifestyle & Habits

Take the time to teach your kids life lessons and enforce them. Take every opportunity to talk openly about things like:

- Buy only what you need.

  We make our kids pay for a portion of their shoes, clothing and experiences — sometimes the whole thing. (Funny how they don't "need" things as badly when they're footing the bill!)

- Expect chores to be done.

  My husband and I don't often shovel, mow, dust, or do dishes. We occasionally help, but our kids mostly do it. We also pay our kids when they do tasks that are above and beyond normal household duties.

- Live a healthy lifestyle.

  Get healthy as a family. Eat right and exercise. Set a great example, and they'll follow.

- Organize together.

  Let your kids have some ownership in helping to define space for their things, errand items, bins for Salvation Army giveaway items, etc.

- Encourage spirituality.

  Say Grace at family dinners, and recite prayers at night.

- Establish traditions.

  Maybe you always have choices of soups on Christmas Eve,

and hide Easter Baskets. Or you have a special birthday hat that the birthday person is required to wear. Make cookies at Hanukkah. Give out May baskets. It doesn't matter much what the traditions are, just that you follow them consistently. Kids find comfort in familiarity, look forward to these traditions, and will remember them forever.

Rally Your Spouse's Support

Men, this section is for your wives, girlfriends or sig others, as we know that we control the atmosphere at home. Sorry. But it's downright true.

Sometime between "I do" and parent/teacher conferences, I've seen many women become cynical, lazy, and downright bratty.

I try not to argue over small stuff. (It's tough, because we're both always right.) I try not to be an exhausted brat. I flirt with him.

Want respect and a better marriage? We hold the key to this, ladies. Be an "old school" wife by doing simple things to make him feel special, and you will get what you want. Cook (or arrange for) dinner every night. Clean the house (or manage the process). Take his car in for an oil change. Rub his feet (jk… I don't do this unless asked, but it sounds good, right?). Encourage him to have some down time or time with friends, just like you need.

Communicate openly. Accept criticism without jumping to the defense. I know when I get stressed, I get defensive and don't take criticism well. But I'm always great at dishing it out. I have to remind myself that I married a man who would would jump in front of a bus for me. Count to ten, soften and listen. Focus on making each other better people.

Of course, all this advice is the perfect scenario in the perfect world. My world is less than perfect, so I still sometimes choose unwisely and bitch. That's why we need to get good at eating humble pie and apologies.

In short, think back to when you were dating. Did you complain to your friends about every nail clipping and manscaped hair? Do you still treat him like you're trying to hook him? You know if you need to make some changes.

You'll find that if you follow these basic rules, your husband will more readily support your efforts and your home will be a happy one.

Be A Spitfire

When learning new information throughout life, it always helps to understand when we can place it in a context. Here is a checklist of additional things I strive to learn and teach my kids over the years, so they have a broader and more cultured frame of reference.

_____ Try new veggies, fruits, and cheeses

_____ States, Capitals, Major Cities & Locations

_____ Countries, Major Cities & Locations

_____ Basic American History Timeline

_____ Basic World History Timeline

_____ Presidents and World Leaders

_____ Renowned Sports Figures

_____ Classic Plays and Movies

_____ Books of The Bible and other Holy Books

Chapter 4

Create More Money and Your Passion for Making It

You're fun. You're organized. Your family is helping out. Now let's get you in a money-making mindset.

Many of the wealthiest people I know started with nothing, learned to budget, educated themselves on creating wealth, and stuck to a disciplined plan.

They didn't start with big money. They practiced discipline in budgeting and saving, and grew from there.

We established a great method for budgeting in the beginning of our marriage 25 years ago. (Remember that I came from a mother who reeeeally knew how to spend? David had to reel that in.) We called it "The Envelope System," and it worked like a charm.

I learned to love budgeting, "finding money," and studying about how to make money work for us… not the other way around. I was developing a money mindset. And the rest would be history.

Establishing Your Budget: "The Envelope System"

Sit down and figure out, based on your total income, how much you can spend on everything you need or want on a monthly basis.

1.   Write down your household monthly income at the top of a sheet of paper. This is what you bring home in paychecks.

2.   Make a list of your essential expenses, making sure you have enough money for:

Mortgage/Rent
Car Payment/s
Taxes
Insurances
Utilities (gas/water/electric)
Credit Card Balances (kudos if you have none!)
Retirement Savings
Business Savings

IMPORTANT: Consider "Savings" to be an essential expense, as no matter what your budget, you always should be planning for the future. This includes maxing out any retirement savings PLUS paying into a savings account at the bank for any early growth or startup business costs (if you're still in these stages).

3.   Consider additional static monthly expenses that are non-essential, and make a list of these. For example:

TV/Internet
Phone Bills
Memberships/Subscriptions

4.   Finally, figure out how much money you have left for remaining monthly living expenses, and divide this remainder

into the 7 main categories below. Get 7 Legal Envelopes, and label each one with a category:

Target/Wal-Mart
Groceries
Kids (if you have kids)
Gas/Transportation
Travel/Entertainment
Pets (if you have pets)
Gifts/Shopping/Miscellaneous

5.   Tweak your budget based on the amount you have left for discretionary "envelope" spending. If you find that you don't have enough for your envelopes, you will have to look at your list of expenses in #3 and tweak or eliminate.

It is of utmost importance to learn to live within your means. In other words, DON'T SPEND WHAT YOU DON'T HAVE.

On this note, you'll notice that there is no category for credit cards. It's very important to put away your credit cards until you are able to stay within your new budget. Store them in a safe place, as you are not allowed to use them except in emergency situations. Even then, you must take the equivalent cash out of an envelope to pay for the charge.

Quick Tip

One of the biggest pitfalls to a successful budget is carrying unnecessary debt. Make it your chief goal to pay off bad debt like credit cards or loans that offer no tax benefit.

Credit card companies will often lower your interest rate if you simply call and ask. Then, make a plan to pay the most you possibly can each month to rid yourself of this debt for good. You may have to get rid of TV or cell phones to work this into your monthly budget. It's THAT important that you get rid of this debt and never acquire it again.

During the early years when we used "The Envelope System," there were months when we ran out of money in the "Target" envelope and had to use money from "Shopping." And there were months when we were flat broke and getting creative with canned foods and leftovers.

The key is: no cheating! We learned very quickly to live within our means. And NEVER did we skip paying our savings account. This is the fund you need to get ahead.

However, we were both working full time, so we were able to keep steadily adding to our envelopes on a monthly basis to enjoy more evenings out and shopping. We increased our monthly envelope allowances to a comfortable amount. We then increased our monthly savings. Only after all this, we allowed ourselves to start using credit cards… keeping good track of what we charged… and knowing that we'd be able to pay the full amount of the bills every month.

Quick Tip

Find an excellent investment advisor to open Qualified Savings Accounts that grow tax-free or offer the best tax advantages.

Ask friends you admire for referrals. Don't be afraid to meet with several before you make a decision with whom to work.

Ask each one to lay out a general plan for you, and you will get a sense for the right fit.

Developing A Money Mindset

The Envelope System empowered me to realize that I'm in total control of spending. It actually became like a game. In the meantime, I educated myself on the benefits of tax write-offs and good investments. (It was in my blood… remember my grandfather and his disdain for taxes?!) David was a successful surgical sales rep, and I was moving up quickly at the ad agency where I worked. Both making great coin, we grew more and more disgusted with how much we paid every year in taxes… crazy amounts!

I considered the benefits of quitting my job and starting a business, like flexibility (especially for when we would have kids) and tax write-offs.

So our budget was on track; I was restless in my job; and we had built our savings. I was having fun with this "finding money" stuff!

It was time to consider what I wanted my future to look like. I knew I wanted to be home for our future kids, but also needed to fulfill my need to always be "out there" using my marketing skills. I loved working for the big ad agency, but knew this wasn't going to fit my master plan. Time to consider going it alone.

It's important to make your work fun and fit into your personal life. Per day, on average, we spend:

- 7 hours sleeping;
- 2 hours cooking & eating;
- 1/2 hour exercising;
- 1/2 hour getting ready.

That leaves 14 hours per day for work and play.

Imagine spending most of those 14 hours per day working on an assembly line. Would you be happy with constant concentration and repetition? Or imagine working as a security officer. Would you be happy interacting with people, standing for long periods of time, and writing reports? How about planning and preparing meals in a restaurant? Serving those meals? Cleaning up after those meals? Selling? Running a company? Running errands for companies? Running an errand running company?

There are so many career choices available today. It's hard to believe that most high school graduates don't even take a class on finding out where their interests lie. They move right into the work force or attend college and pray they fall into a major that captures their interest. They hope to stumble into a career that doesn't bore them day in and day out for 40+ years.

The majority of people in the work force have little or no control over their work lives. They often feel frantic, out of balance, and that they're doing nothing well… like they're just hanging on to get by.

Success in work is not all about money. It's about controlling your own destiny and balance. Work at doing what you love, and balance this with play with the people you love. Aren't we all ultimately in control of our own actions and their resulting feelings? Of course! It only makes sense that the more you act to improve your life, the more you'll enjoy every aspect of it.

Now that you're on the path to financial independence, you can tackle this ultimate control and balance. True Zen.

If you don't love every aspect of your life, do what you can to change that. Now. I'm obviously not recommending an abrupt move to Vegas or sending the kids to boarding school. But there are areas of your life you can start with.

I encourage you to start that business you've been dreaming about (or think bigger to grow the one you've already got). Not only will you realize additional income and tax savings, but also you gain a flexible schedule and freedom.

I realized very quickly when I hit a "glass ceiling" at the big ad agency that I'd be in my current position as the youngest ever with my title for a long time, and would only move on to more work hours and time away from family.

Having a degree from the best University in my specialty at the time (Go Jayhawks!), and training in excellent planning and management, I made great connections and learned first-hand how to get just about anything done in marketing (and if I didn't know, I knew who to call). Add all this to my dream for flexibility, tax savings, and the fact that I had the cash to get started. All I needed was courage.

Courage. Hmmm. I grew up in a business family. I played business whenever I got the chance as a little girl (making my little sister be the customer). I made the most ad sales in history for our middle school yearbook. I revamped the ad section of my high school newspaper. I grew my college ad agency. I started as an intern and worked my way up. Was that enough to give me credibility? I was only 25 then. Was

I too young to be so bold and courageous as to think business owners and execs would take marketing advice from little me?

Looking back today after 25 years of decision-making and risk-taking, I now realize one of my defining moments when I found my courage and validation. One day at the big ad agency, just after losing a large client and knowing layoffs were eminent, I let my restlessness for promotion trump all logic or concern about losing my job. See, I was just an intern, along with about 6 others. I knew we'd be the first to go. So with nothing to lose, what did I do? I gathered up all the nerve I could muster and marched into the VP-Director of Account Services office and told him (heart thumping): "Steve, although I really appreciate all the experience I've gained and love working at this agency, I'm restless for more responsibility. If you don't promote me soon, I will be leaving." I had just handed them one for the chopping block! You know what happened one week later? Several people lost their jobs, including the interns, and I was promoted. Did I feel guilty? A little. Did this feeling last? Hell, no! I dove right into the next challenge, like I always do.

Three years later, I made the courageous decision to quit and start my own business. Sure it was scary, but fast forward two years to $2 million in billings, and my fear was gone.

After building my own agency to $2 million, my husband and I relocated to northern Wisconsin, where we knew we wanted to raise our future family. I knew I was able to grow a business and adapt to work from anywhere. And he could sell from anywhere, as long as he was producing.

We made our work fit the lifestyle we wanted.

Wanting to raise children in a small town, we started our family, which brought new and welcome business challenges. I started working with smaller and local clients, and reached out via the internet to work with more clients throughout the U.S., in the UK and in Canada. I also enjoy speaking about marketing to groups and conducting virtual seminars. It's not the same as working with the big, multi-nationals I once did, but it works in our lifestyle... and that's most important.

You see, entrepreneurialism is contagious. The simple act of starting a small business opened my mind and catapulted my skill set to take on so much more as the years went on.

I've since expanded to diversify our investments, investing in properties and building a business around this, too. I sit on non-profit boards and volunteer.

This information is not included here to brag, but to motivate you to go get your dream. Remember we started with skinny envelopes!

It was a step-by-step process that involved quitting my job, jumping off a small cliff, prayer, and a great support system. Now, the leaps get bigger every time, but I'm always more and more comfortable with the jump.

Be A Spitfire

Dream Big!

Create your vision for success. Imagine yourself on a typically great day 3 – 5 years from now. How is your work? What are you wearing, driving, eating? Who are you with? Describe this dream day in detail. Then, read on, and go get it!

Today was a very good day...

_____

_____

_____

_____

_____

_____

_____

_____

_____

_____

_____

_____

_____

Thanks to my dear friend and fellow marketer,
Leslie Hamp, for this exercise.

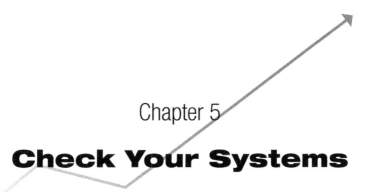

Chapter 5

Check Your Systems

My new friend, this is where the rubber hits the road. You've chosen the entrepreneurial route to having your cake and eating it too. (Translation: having a life of joy in building wealth and feeding your passion.) As much as you can adopt great habits and attitudes, you must create systems that ensure your success.

Remember from the beginning of this book that my secrets are simple. Let's expand on them here to energize you, fortify you and, most importantly, set you up for success.

1. **You must challenge yourself.**

My grandfather said "It's not what you do from 9:00 — 5:00 that matters most. It's what you do from 5:00 — 9:00." In other words, those who put forth more effort, get more.

Lesson: Work very smart during the time you allot.

He also said "I'd love to buy you for what you're really worth, and sell you for what you think you're worth."

Lesson: Gain the courage to take on the world, but always remember you're but a tiny specimen on the world map.

My father-in-law, Jim George, read people better than anyone. He could meet you and peg you with 99% accuracy as successful, an idiot, a bum, insincere... the list is long.

Lesson: Shut up and listen, trust your instincts, and then act accordingly.

Takeaway from these lessons:

Have Genuine Purpose. Few businesses succeed without an underlying purpose-driven cause. And the leaders of these companies are well-grounded in their chosen faith, steadfast in their decision-making, and able to recognize the difference between temporary setback and failure. In every business decision you make, consult your genuine purpose, and you can't go wrong.

A couple examples of excellent purpose-driven companies:

• Trilliant Surgical, LLP

  Trilliant Surgical, which happens to be my husband's company, was founded on the premise that podiatric surgeons, some of the nicest and most fun in the surgical industry, deserved to have a company that was dedicated to developing and manufacturing products solely (no pun intended) for their use.

• Seventh Generation

  Seventh Generation is an organic supply company that walks its talk. They're truly committed to improving the environment. For example, encouraging customers to line-dry clothes, when you sell a dryer sheet product, might be seen as cannibalization of sales by other companies. Instead, new and loyal customers keep coming back because of their candid and trust-building advice.

2. **You must take risks.**

When I was in high school, my mom got her real estate license, earned additional certifications, bought land, subdivided it, and developed it for profit.

Lesson: You're not getting any younger. Get the tools you need, and then take the leap. Let your kids see you do what it takes.

My friend, Nancy Anderson, challenged me to truly diversify when investing. I'll never forget the day she told me "I won't take any more of your money. You need to do something else."

Lesson: Think outside your comfort zone.

Takeaway from these lessons:

Take risks. Be smart. But take risks. No one ever has realized success without risk. Remember that only 2% of women and 5% of men will ever take the risk of a startup. You're in an small minority of risk-takers. Be a smart one.

When considering risking money, make sure it's savings that are earmarked for company use and growth. Don't mix business and personal funds. Take time to thoughtfully consider the funds you will need for success. Put business earnings and/or personal savings into a business account for this purpose. Do not tap into personal funds beyond this.

Also, have enough stashed away in your personal accounts to pay bills during a dry spell.

Be realistic with your projections, and plan to raise capital if necessary.

Then, remember that if you don't jump, you stay in place. Muster the courage, and take the leap!

Quick Tip

Remind yourself that most people will poke holes in projects and talk a big game, but only 12% of American adults are involved in a startup business (source: "Forbes Magazine"). And only 30% of those businesses are women-owned. So the next time you're in a room with 50 women, look around. Consider which one may have the balls to start a business like you do! Men, when you're in a room of 50, look around and consider which three of them have the courage that you do.

3. **You must stay grounded.**

My dad is a very grounded and reliable guy. I remember him ripping a borrowed Judy Blume book titled "Forever" in half when he found out I was reading it after being told not to.

Lesson: Have a good set of values. Earn respect and follow through.

I can get so focused on tasks that I neglect feelings. My kids help me remember this daily.

Lesson: Make sure you pour some heart into what you're doing.

Takeaway from these lessons:

As success mounts, you will need to realize more time and expertise. Use your grounded purpose, good judgment, and income or savings you've earmarked for growth to put the right people in place to ensure less stress and the ability to focus on what you enjoy and do best.

Not everyone is your friend. Surround yourself with positive people who encourage you to move forward. People who do the right thing. People who like to have fun and encourage you to express yourself genuinely. If your friends don't fit this description, dump them.

Get off Facebook, Instagram, Snapchat, or whatever other currently popular social media may be sucking your time.

Consider hiring help. This may be as simple as finding someone to help with housework. Or a coach to keep you on track. It's always good to have an excellent accountant… one who understands the benefits of owning a business. My support system now includes my attorney, my accountant, freelancers, investment advisors, real estate agents, property managers, and an administrative assistant. And, of course, great friends and family.

And finally, take a look around. Does your business reflect who you are? Does it do everything to entice the right customers and keep them? Is your front entrance welcoming? Are people greeted with friendliness and smiles? Are your trucks clean? Imagine you're a customer walking in the door (or calling to inquire), and "walk" through your process. Are there any hiccups? Fix them!

4. **You must be real.**

My husband, David, is funny, heart-felt, candid (aka Greek), and arguably THE biggest challenge anyone could encounter. He will hands-down make you a better person (if you are willing to put up with his crap).

Lesson: Have an opinion, and don't be afraid to use it. Don't dance around issues. Say "no" when you should.

I'll add another one of my favorite quotes here (by another brilliant, yet unknown, author): "Don't be upset with the results you get from the work you didn't put in."

Takeaway from these lessons:

The biggest mistake I see in business ownership is lack of knowing how to transition from working IN your business to working ON your business. In other words, many business owners love their trade, but they realize that they do not love running a business related to their trade. Suddenly, they're wearing more "hats" and aren't able to do the actual work they love full-time.

If you find yourself among this group, be honest with yourself. Realize that you may have to give more thought to performing some tasks that you don't especially love. Or say "no" to tasks that drain you, and budget for hiring help.

Life's too long to hate your work… and it's too short to love it too much. Consider budgeting for people or services to handle the aspects of your business that you dread or are not a whiz at doing. The investment may be justified by freeing up your time to enjoy greater happiness and a smoother running business.

Considering the following general business task categories, and quantify the energy you have around completing tasks in these categories by rating it:

1 = Love It!
2 = It's OK.
3 = Hate It!

_____ Management

_____ Product Development

_____ Office Administration/Bookkeeping

_____ Marketing

_____ Sales

_____ Customer Service/Fulfillment

Plan to delegate/hire out the tasks that are marked with a "3" as soon as your budget allows, then those marked "2."

As a small business owner, you wear many "hats" while running your business. Some of the tasks you perform are more fun than others. Whether you find happiness working on your business' assembly line, selling, interacting with diners, or balancing the books — plan for happiness by doing what you choose to do.

5. **Coffee, healthy living, and excellent red wine.**

Rev up your day, eat smart, exercise, and unwind at night.

Lesson: Take care of yourself. Be as healthy as you can to stay on top of your game and enjoy it all!

Takeaway from this lesson:

As a business owner, you are in control of your work life. If you're happy with work, other things seem to fall into place. Love your work, and it feels like play. Considering work and the time spent with family and friends — that's 14 hours of fun every day!

Develop healthy habits. Exercise. Eat well. Connect daily with your spouse/sig other, your kids, and your friends & employees. This is how you'll keep a pulse on your life. Address any feelings of unbalance immediately, so issues stay small or go away.

Choose wisely who you allow into your circle, thus affecting your life in positive ways, and problem-solving will be easy. If you choose wisely to INVEST your time rather than SPEND it, you will come out on top. Stay focused on your mission for success.

Be A Spitfire

Identify your barriers to success, and break through them.

Rate yourself in the following categories on a scale of 1 - 5 ("1" means no concern, and "5" means this is a potential problem area for you.)

Keep these barriers in mind when considering support you may need in your business.

_____ Lack of business acumen or knowledge
           of next steps

_____ Procrastination, lack of momentum
           or accountability

_____ Fear of rejection or failure

_____ Worry about credibility, lack of skills
           or expertise

_____ Not knowing how to market, sell
           or close a sale

_____ Shyness or apprehension of "putting
           yourself out there"

_____ Worry about delivering on your word
           or fulfilling orders

_____ Fear of becoming too busy or successful

Chapter 6

Write Your Plan for Unstoppable Success

Write Your Spitfire Marketing Plan

Yes, I have worked with all types and sizes of businesses since 1994, helping them launch and grow. I've done countless logos, taglines, full-scale international marketing plans and long-term business projections.

I love it all. But you don't need it all. I wrote this book to help you focus on only what you need to move forward quickly and easily.

That's why I call this your "Spitfire Marketing Plan." It focuses your efforts on only what you need to figure out, so you're empowered to take action.

Assuming you've nailed the logistics of setting up and starting your chosen business at this point, and that you're on track to tweak operations to fit your dreams... you need to get more money coming in.

Let's write your plan to market your dream.

Define your Target Audience.

Who wants and needs what you have to offer? The only wrong answer is "everyone." If you're a pediatrician, you may see infants and children. Are they your target audience? No! They are your patients, but it's the parents you need to connect with to get the kids in your door.

And it's not just any parents – it's a definite group of parents.

In marketing, you get a lot more "bang for your buck" if you focus your efforts and spending on a well-defined group of people that you enjoy working with. The better you define this group, the more effective your marketing can be.

Set your sights on working with only those clients who bring out your very best – people whose problems and challenges you relate to, people who need and appreciate your products or services, people who are fun to work with!

When you work with your ideal customer or client, your brilliance will show and you'll have more fun.

How do you define your ideal customer? Consider a few of your best clients, and write down their demographics - their age, gender, education level, profession, income, marital status, parental status, life stage. If you work in business-to-business, consider the type of business, structure, age, sales, and size.

Expand on this information by considering their lifestyles.

Close your eyes and walk through their day. What do they eat for breakfast? What kind of car do they drive? Where do they shop? How do they "treat" themselves? What do they value most?

Describe your core target below. This information will be very valuable in helping you to determine where to focus your marketing efforts.

_____

_____

_____

_____

_____

_____

_____

_____

_____

<u>Determine what makes you most unique.</u>

What is the one most unique strength your business offers above any competition? Your Point of Difference is the one, positive trait your brand possesses that would not be duplicated with success by any competing brand.

In order to create a differentiation that won't be imitated, you have to think beyond the things that are considered important in your brand's category.

A successful differentiation is not imitated by your competitors, even though it brings you unmistakable success with consumers. Although it may be easy for your competitors to imitate, it would be stupid for them to try.

Small businesses are easily adapted, so they have an excellent opportunity to differentiate right out of the gate. Here are some examples of excellent differentiation by larger businesses:

- UPS brown trucks

- Tiffany's blue gift boxes

- Lush organic handmade cosmetics

- Airstream RV's iconic shape

- Cinnabon's iconic smell

Point of Difference is the one, positive trait a given brand possesses that would not be duplicated with success by any competing brand.

The companies that have succeeded in maintaining their differentiation over the years and weren't imitated — even though they were making tremendous profits — are those that keep innovating while keeping their differentiation top-of-mind.

Let's determine your business' most unique trait - its Point of Difference.

1.   On the next page, you will see 2 circles. The circle on the left is all about YOU. Write what's unique about your company or products… the things you will do best. For example, maybe you want to make the best cheesecakes. But how will they be different? Are they completely handmade? Do you deliver your cheesecakes? So, a couple of things you'd answer in this section could be: "Handmade" and "Delivery."

2.   The circle on the right is all about YOUR CUSTOMER. Write what you know to be true about their specific needs that you can fulfill. Hint: look back at your definition of your Target Audience,

and consider what you wrote about their likes, dislikes, and habits, or when walking a day in their shoes. For example, maybe your Target Audience is busy women who love to entertain, doing their own cooking. So, you could write "busy women" and "great cook" and "entertain" in this section.

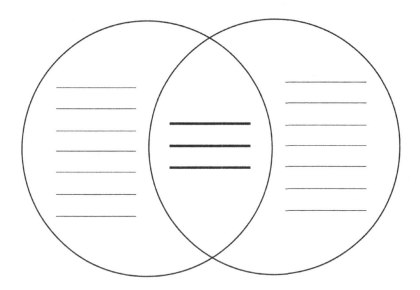

What similarities do you see in both circles – similarities between unique things you offer and the needs and desires of your Target Audience? Write the one statement that appears strongest in the middle of the circles. In this example, you might write in the middle: "handmade and delivered to you on your platter."

See how your business can blossom over it's competition from just this one statement? Maybe you deliver cheesecakes that are easily transferred to the owner's platter, so they can pass it off as their own. Genius!

This is your Point of Difference. Most business owners have never identified this in a meaningful and calculated way. Instead, their brands remain at parity or die without it.

You, however, have now captured that one, elusive trait that breathes life and great growth potential into your brand.

Can you see how it will help you with your marketing messages?

Memorize it. Live it. Shout it from the mountain tops!

<u>Write your 10-Second Interview.</u>

If I were to approach you right now and ask you to describe your company, could you convey its most important benefits in 10 seconds?

Benefits are not what you offer. Benefits consider what you offer, and go further… answering how your offerings help your Target Audience, by making them smarter, faster, richer, safer…

Here are some examples of benefit-driven statements. These all are great starts when writing a 10-Second Interview:

- "We streamline efforts and increase profits for home-based businesses."

- "We take the nightmare out of bookkeeping."

- "We give you a good night's sleep."

- "We create nutritious meals for family dinners."

Now, pretend Oprah Winfrey ran into you at a party, had done a little field work, and was considering investing in your company. You have 10 seconds to "WOW" her. Ready? Go!

If you can't give Oprah a great understanding of what your company is all about without boring her, no one else can!

Considering your work to this point, write your 10-Second Interview now. Below is a guide to get your started:

We work with _____ (target audience) who struggle with _____ (challenge your target faces that you solve) and would like _____ (results/benefits).

What makes us different from other _____ (your business category) is that we _____ (your solution).

Essentially, we are unique because we _____ (Point of Difference).

Create your Tagline.

This will require some creative thinking, so you might need to carve out some quiet time when you're feeling creative.

Your tagline is one phrase – included in all your marketing – that should get to the heart of what's important to your Target Audience.

Your tagline should capture the "spirit" of what you offer, while promoting your Point of Difference.

Some historically great examples:

- "What can brown do for you?" (UPS)

- "Just Do It" (Nike)

- "Think different." (Apple)

- "Can you hear me now? Good." (Verizon)

- "Because You're Worth It" (L'Oreal)

- "Got milk?" (California Milk Board)

- "We try harder." (Avis)

- "Betcha can't eat just one." (Lay's)

- "The Ultimate Driving Machine" (BMW)

- "Melts in your mouth, not in your hand" (M&M's)

- "Don't leave home without it." (AMEX)

Brainstorm and consider your Tagline here:

_____

_____

_____

Quick Tip

This part can get tough for even the most seasoned business owners and marketers. Please please please feel free to contact us if you are stuck and need a boost, or want help with this whole thing. Seriously!
www.SpitfirePromotionGroup.com

What is your Creative Direction?

The job of a highly effective brand is to speak to one very targeted audience. When developing marketing materials, you will visualize and speak directly to the person you described as your Target Audience.

You've created your Tagline. You know your Point of Difference. Now consider how you can convey these things through design and message.

Write copy for your marketing materials in a compelling message that:

- Speaks to your strengths

- Makes a promise you are willing to keep

- Positions your company in a positive way

- Meets the needs of your Target Audience

- Helps you meet your business objectives

Try writing some sentences for your advertising message here:

_____

_____

_____

_____

_____

_____

_____

Also consider your overall look. Look at competitors' marketing pieces and other designs that you like and think would convey the "feel" of your company.

- What are your colors?

- Do you have an icon (or symbol) that defines your brand?

- A certain shape?

- How about a sound or smell?

- What words describe your business and its attributes?

Considering if you had to tell a design professional to put together an ad for your company, write your overall direction for designing your marketing here:

_____

_____

_____

_____

_____

_____

_____

Define your Top 5 Marketing Strategies.

People don't buy products or services; they buy solutions to their problems. You want to figure out the best places to spend your marketing efforts and dollars in order to pull customers in like a magnet.

Not all ideas listed here may be necessary for your business, but they should be considered.

I encourage only 5 strategies at a time simply because I want you to be realistic, focusing on your best strategies only, and carry them out really well. As you become a more seasoned business owner, you will determine what works best and be able to add strategies to your list.

From the categories and examples below, make a list of only the Top 5 best marketing activities that you will use to grow business. (If an activity is not ongoing, be sure to replace it with another good idea once it's accomplished.)

•   Identity Pieces to consider:

These "out-of-the-gate" pieces can be created and printed quickly.

Examples are:

Business cards
Letterhead & envelopes
Brochures
Flyers
Signage (in-store, outside, vehicle)
Coupon to inspire buyers
Giveaways (pens, mugs, t-shirts, free how-to manual)

•   Online Marketing options to consider:

Online marketing may require expertise to set up, but often is structurally maintenance-free once it's done correctly. Whatever you do online, be sure to gain training on how to make your own updates, send your own messages, and post your own information… all of which will save you money.

Here are examples:

Website or web page

Blog (for writing and cataloguing relevant business-related information)

Social Media
    Facebook, Instagram, Twitter, etc.

Customized apps for mobile devices

Online banner & pop-up ads

These are strategically placed paid ads on sites that your Target Audience visits, that link back to your web site.

Shared links

Again, think strategically about where your Target Audience visits, and approach those site owners about swapping links... placing a link to your site on their site, while you place an ad for them on yours.

E-commerce

Selling online directly or on other sites

• Direct Marketing options to consider:

Although more time consuming, marketing directly to customers is more personal and makes success tracking easy. A few examples are:

Mass mailings

Create a general mailing piece to get the message out to several households or businesses (usually 500+). I've done mass mailings to 2 million households in the past, and there are lots of cost savings to be had in bulk; however, even though these can be "personalized," you lose the personal touch. A highly targeted mailing list can be purchased from a reputable list company.

Newsletter

Chock this full of great advice, and send it monthly or quarterly. Be sure that you have the time to adhere to whatever mailing schedule you establish.

Holiday cards

Phone calls

Have a script ready, and practice it, so you know exactly what you want to communicate. Don't forget a "call to action," asking them for business. Phone numbers can be obtained easily by asking clients or having them drop in a business card for a drawing. Or, all types of highly targeted contact information can be purchased from list companies.

Email campaign

Collect e-mails and send timely information; however, don't become a pest by e-mailing too often.

- Collaborations

Collaboration (aka "partnering" or "fusion marketing") involves bringing together <u>non-competing companies</u> with:
— the same target audience,
— the same market area, and
— the same attitude... to share in marketing efforts.

I love collaborative marketing because it's fun, and the right collaborations deliver big impact & high returns at a fraction of the cost.

You can get as involved as you want with this. Some great examples (large and small) using our clients are:

<u>Large-scale Example</u>

"Superior Snow"

This was a promotion for northern Michigan ski areas to lure avid skiing families in the Midwest to the area by using several marketing strategies, including media, direct mail, online ads, and coupons in retail locations.

Coca-Cola contributed in exchange for ski and lodging packages by providing special cans marked with "you win" in vending machines and convenience stores. Subaru contributed in exchange for ski and lodging packages in their dealerships by advertising a free lift ticket with a test drive. Radio, TV and print media contributed by Coke, plus a "Ski Magazine" feature story, rounded out the perfect media mix.

This involved six marketing partners comprised of 4 ski resorts, Coca-Cola and Subaru (plus regional McDonald's, Burger King and 18 more local businesses that provided a coupon sheet to all families that made the trip).

Approximate Cost: $250 for each local partner; average $50,000 for each anchor partner (Subaru, Coca-Cola, and the ski areas).

The average rate of return: 3.8% on high ticket items (Subaru ran out of offers early!); 18%+ on local tie-ins.

Mid-scale Example

"Birthday Club"

A direct marketing piece with birthday deals was mailed to 60,000 Minneapolis/St. Paul households with children the month prior to their birthdays, tied in with University of Minnesota Athletics to increase awareness of their new Kids Club. Radio Disney and Minnesota Sports Channel TV spots supplemented in a media plan. Brochures also were placed in 50+ retail locations, mostly in Target Stores.

There were 13 marketing partners in total (7 on the mailing piece), and rate of return on the coupons offered was excellent: 12-38%.

Approximate Cost: $6,000 for each mailing partner (only 10¢ per piece).

Small-scale Example

"Just Too Busy"

Virtual Assistant firm, Just Too Busy, of the UK was looking to increase its client base from three to a dozen. We paired Just Too Busy with "The Women's Marketing Forum" in London, where Alex Greer, owner, spoke on various topics. She filled her client roster within one week.

You see, great collaborations offer a win-win-win situation. You benefit. Your partner/s benefit. Your clients benefit. You gotta love that!

- Media Advertising

Big media advertising is a comparatively pricey option, so it makes sense only if you have a more general target audience and can afford it. Examples are:

Television
Radio
Print (newspaper, magazine, billboards, bus benches)

There are smaller, more niched options like boutique publications, that are highly targeted. Some of these might make better sense for reaching your defined target more affordably. Look at their target audience information to make sure it matches up with who you are trying to reach.

- Public Relations

Getting out in the public is a great way to spread the word about your business. Again, think strategically about where your time and efforts are best spent. Here are some ideas:

Join groups.

Write an article, and ask if a chosen targeted publication will print it. This is, of course, up to their discretion, but it's a great way to establish yourself as an expert and get some free publicity. NOTE: Be sure to keep the article informative. Don't sell, as then it appears to be an ad. Just be sure to put your name, company name, and contact information at the end of the article (soft sell ;)

Do radio or TV interviews.

Offer to speak as an expert at conferences.

Plan or sponsor events that your target audience will be attending.

- BIG BUZZ Guerrilla Marketing Idea

Guerrilla Marketing is another favorite strategy for me. Guerrilla Marketing is excellent for small businesses because it is <u>low cost</u> and just requires:
– Time,
– Energy, and
– Imagination.

Put the time in with a group of friends to brainstorm some fun, off-the-wall strategies to get people's attention. Then, get their help with implementation.

Do something fascinating, and people will talk about it. Keep it simple, so your fun message is easy to transmit from one person to the next.

Some of my favorites:

A ski resort wanted more local skiers, so they placed skier cutouts on snow-covered car windshields parked on local streets. The cutouts had the name of the resort and a lift ticket discount coupon.

This "Ugly Betty" promotion by a facialist put paper bags with eye-hole cutouts over street signs. The bags promoted a makeover. (This one's clever, but I'd be sure to check on legality first!)

A small grill retailer placed spatulas next to city street sewer grates, saying: "Need a new barbecue?

Call…"

A hair studio put signs under bushes: "Need a trim?

Call…"

And my all-time FAVORITE (oh, how I wish I could say I came up with this one!):

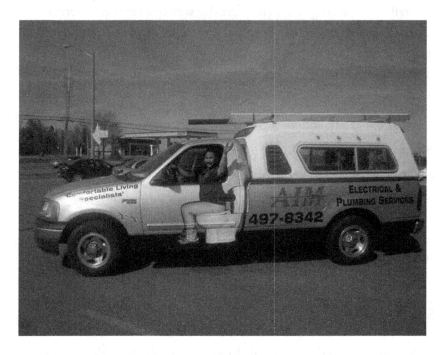

Copyright 2017 AIM Electrical & Plumbing

Now, considering the categories above and all the options within them, write only your Top 5 Marketing Strategies here:

1. _____

_____

2. _____

_____

3. _____

_____

4. _____

_____

5. _____

_____

Sales process step-by-steps

How will you convert strangers to prospects to customers to loyalists?
Your goal is to create not just customers, but loyalists that keep
coming back to you over and over again. These are the people that
will love your brand so much that they market for you.

Determine your sales process, starting with how you will find your
Target Audience, all the way through how you plan to keep them
loyal to your business.

1. Turn strangers into prospects. Keeping in mind that most
    people need to hear from you 7-10 times before they will even
    consider buying, in what ways will you make initial contact,
    or make your Target Audience aware of your offerings?

_____

_____

_____

_____

_____

_____

2. Turn prospects into customers. Once you make your Target Audience aware of you, what will you entice them with to walk in your door or to try your product or service?

_____

_____

_____

_____

_____

_____

3. Turn customers into loyalists. Don't forget marketing to your loyalists, your best customers. Ask for referrals, upsell them into an exclusive membership, etc. Just remember that the sale doesn't stop at the sale! How will you make customers love your brand so much that they want to keep coming back and tell their friends about you?

_____

_____

_____

_____

_____

_____

Be A Spitfire

Live the "80/20 Rule!"

Success is so much easier to obtain when you understand and apply the 80/20 Rule to most everything in life! The 80/20 Rule states that 80% of results come from 20% of efforts. Here are some general examples to get you thinking:

• 80% of revenues come from 20% of customers

• 80% of your interruptions come from 20% of your people

• 80% of your calls are to 20% of the people in your address book

• 80% of a company's output is created by 20% of its employees

• 80% of your productivity is during 20% of your working hours

• 80% of your website traffic comes from 20% of its pages

• 80% of what you wear takes up 20% of your closet

Streamline. Focus. And make life easier.

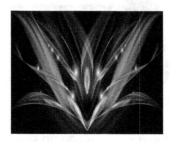

Fellow Spitfire, it's time to hit the ground running! You've accomplished a ton. Take the next step... and the next... and the next. Enjoy your new fun and happiness along the way. You are an unstoppable Spitfire!

And remember, we'd love to hear from you about — or help you with — your journey: www.SpitfirePromotionGroup.com.

Here's to Your Success!

Printed in the United States
By Bookmasters